Illuminated

A JOURNAL FOR
YOUR TAROT PRACTICE

CAITLIN KEEGAN

CLARKSON POTTER/PUBLISHERS
NEW YORK

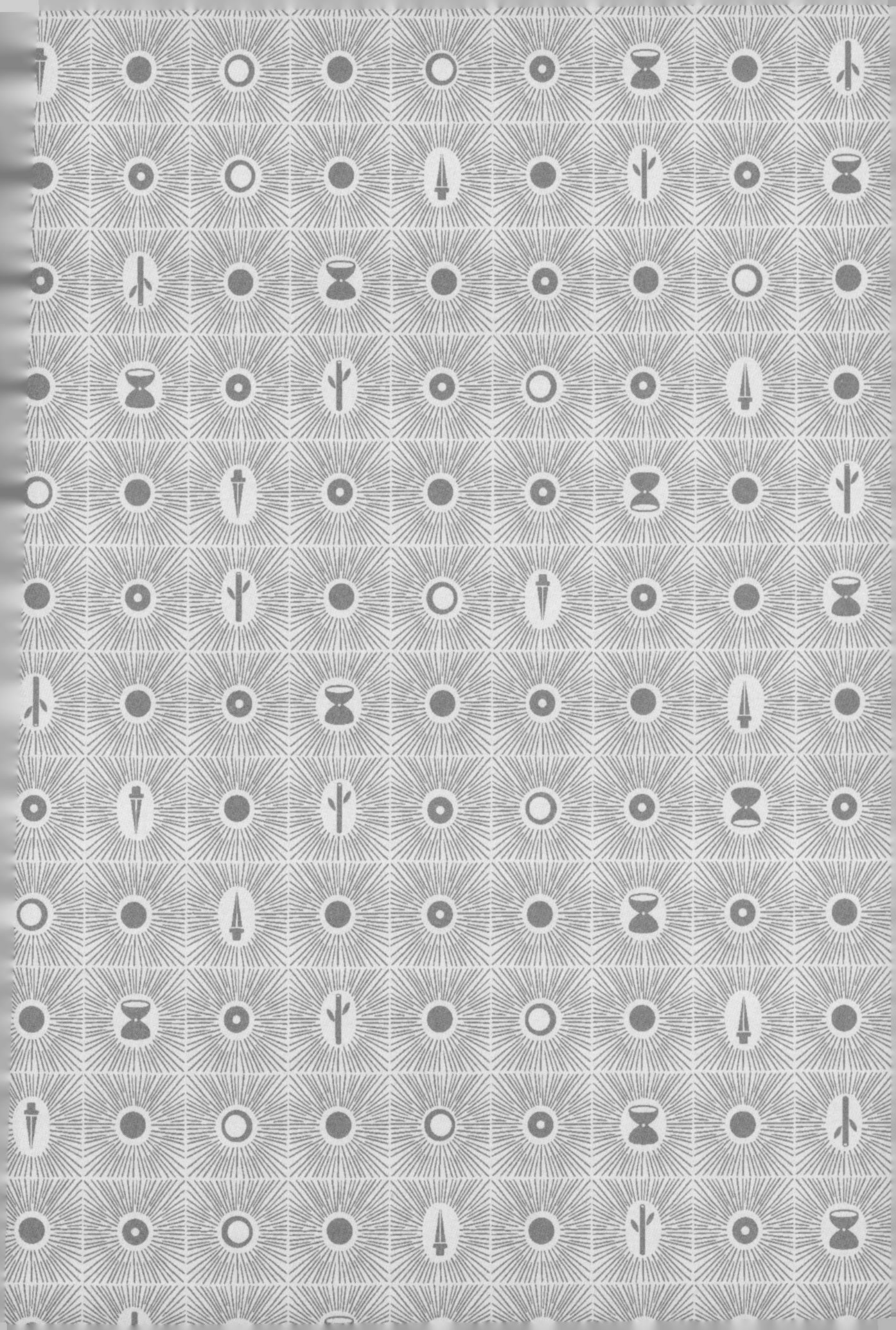

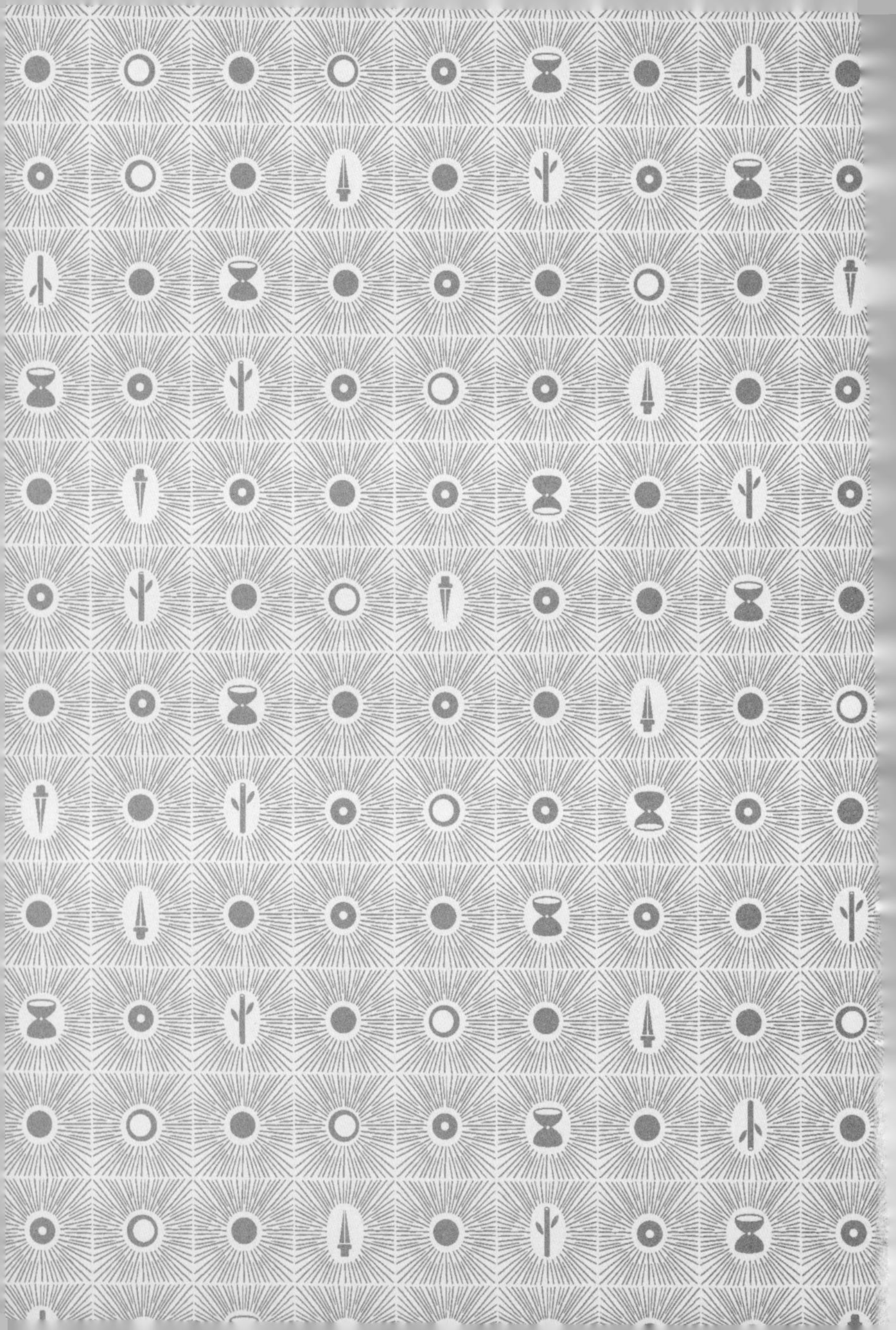

TAROT CAN BE
A POWERFUL TOOL
FOR ILLUMINATING
THE PRESENT.

TAROT CANNOT PREDICT THE FUTURE, BUT IT SPARKS NEW IDEAS AND CLEARS NEW PATHS.

A regular practice helps us develop intuition, set intentions, make decisions, and clarify perspectives.

The history of tarot is long, varied, and somewhat mysterious. Tarot-like games and divination systems have appeared across cultures and regions beginning as early as the ninth century (or as "recently" as the fifteenth century, depending on which scholars you consult). Tarot's unique symbolism is constantly being reinterpreted for new audiences and changing times, making every deck a new dialect of an old language.

My own interest in tarot started in middle school. Interpreting the cards felt like putting together an intriguing visual puzzle. I continued to be interested in tarot well into art school, where I studied illustration and even created a tarot-based game. Years later, I was seeing a therapist for the first time, and, in an early session, she asked me to talk about my own artwork as a way to access deeper issues and feelings. I understood then that image interpretation was one way of clarifying and externalizing unacknowledged emotion. This experience led me to think about tarot in a psychological context. I've since learned that some therapists do, in fact, use tarot as a tool in their sessions.

Up to this point, tarot had fascinated me, but I could never fully grasp what to do with it. When I realized tarot could be used for something other than predicting the future, I committed to learning more about it. At the same time, therapy had become an important agent of change in my life, and I wondered if I could contribute to therapeutic practice through my work as an illustrator. The process of studying tarot inspired me to create *The Illuminated Tarot*: a fully illustrated tarot and playing card deck that is designed to be read intuitively.

Art is both a universal language and a highly personal one. Tarot imagery harnesses this dichotomy, making a tarot deck an accessible and endlessly adaptable tool. In his book *Tarot and Psychology*, Arthur Rosengarten compares reading tarot to analyzing a dream. The advantage that tarot has over dream interpretation, he says, is that all of the imagery is right in front of us; it does not disappear when we wake up. Like dream analysis, tarot readings hint at things just below the surface; intuitive thoughts that have not yet broken through to our consciousness. When I read for myself, I usually feel that the cards either reaffirm something I already know or point me toward a doorway I had not considered. A tarot deck can be a powerful tool for getting in touch with your intuition and writing about the cards amplifies that power. A tarot journal is a record of growth and change over time; it is a reminder of where we've been and a map to where we're going. I hope this journal will help you use tarot for affirmation and discovery.

CHOOSING A DECK

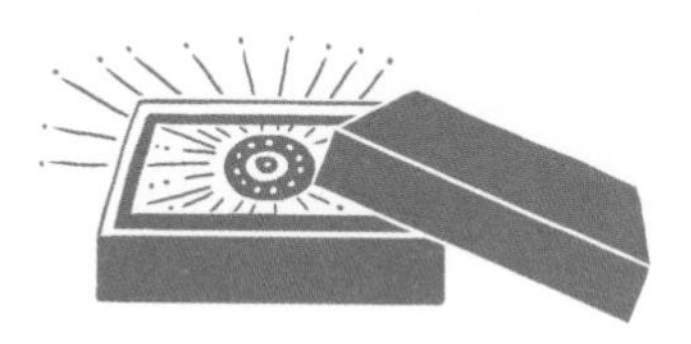

Finding a deck that resonates with you is the key to meaningful readings—especially for beginners. A good way to select a deck is to pick up a few cards at random and interpret them intuitively, not referring to the guidebook at all. The more intuitively you are able to respond to your deck, the easier and more meaningful your readings will be.

The range of tarot and oracle decks in the world is a testament to both the resonance and the flexibility of the tarot system. That said, there are a few prevailing styles within tarot:

♦ THE RIDER-WAITE-SMITH DECK ♦

The most commonly referenced deck, the Rider-Waite-Smith deck, was illustrated by Pamela Colman Smith in collaboration with Arthur Edward Waite. The Rider-Waite-Smith deck has seventy-eight fully illustrated cards: twenty-two Major Arcana and fifty-six Minor Arcana. A number of modern decks are reinterpretations of the Rider-Waite-Smith deck, due to the wide range of symbolism in Smith's now-iconic illustrations. Her influences include ancient Egypt, Greek mythology, Christianity, and alchemy.

♦ TAROT DE MARSEILLES ♦
AND OTHER PLAYING CARD–INFLUENCED DECKS

The first known tarot decks were used for card games. The Italian Visconti-Sforza decks and the French Tarot de Marseilles both date back to the fifteenth century and are comprised of seventy-eight cards, with the numbered Minor Arcana cards designed like playing cards.

♦ THE THOTH DECK ♦

The Thoth deck, created by Aleister Crowley and illustrated by Lady Frieda Harris, deviates from other deck formats in a few ways: Strength is called Lust, Temperance has been renamed Art, Judgment is called the Aeon, and the World becomes the Universe. The court cards are the Knight, Queen, Prince, and Princess.

♦ ORACLE DECKS ♦

Decks that do not have seventy-eight cards are usually referred to as oracle decks. Oracle decks are more free-form: they can have any number of cards, any underlying structure, and a set of meanings that may vary from one of the aforementioned tarot traditions.

TIPS FOR STRENGTHENING YOUR INTUITION

Reading tarot is an art, not a science; that is the beauty of this system. A guidebook can be helpful, but you can (and should!) try to interpret the images yourself. Here are a few ways to add richness and dimension to your readings:

1. **Understand the history and symbolism of the deck you're using.** If the illustrations in your deck are informed by a specific symbolic, philosophical, or religious tradition, a solid understanding of that tradition will add depth to your readings.

2. **Understand what the suit, numbers, and court positions represent.** A familiarity with the traditional meanings for each suit, number, and court position can be helpful when reading your cards. Take a look at the chart in the Reference Pages section for more.

3. **Decide if you want to read with reversals.** Some readers use reversals, others do not. **Reversals** are when a card is laid out upside down rather than right side up. In this position, the card takes on different meanings and attributes. You may decide that this extra layer of meaning is helpful, or you may find it confusing. Trust your instincts.

REVERSALS

Reading reversed cards is not essential, but some readers find that it adds valuable detail. Here are a few ways of interpreting reversed cards.

♦ BLOCKED ENERGY ♦

The energy of the card is not properly manifesting itself. **EXAMPLE:** If the upright Lovers card asks *What shared vision is essential in my relationship?* the reversed Lovers card might ask *What is preventing me from finding a shared vision in my relationship?*

♦ INTERNALIZED ENERGY ♦

The card refers to internal, not external concerns. **EXAMPLE:** If the upright Judgment card asks *How can I forgive?* the reversed Judgment card might ask *How can I forgive myself?*

♦ INVERTED IMAGERY ♦

The card image is interpreted upside down. **EXAMPLE:** If the Ten of Swords depicts a figure laying face-down with ten swords in their back, asking *What do I need to accept?* the reversed image might look like the ten swords are falling out of the figure's back, asking *What do I need to release?*

♦ OPPOSITE MEANING ♦

The reversed card takes on the opposite meaning of the upright card. **EXAMPLE:** If the Emperor asks, *How can I exert influence?* the reversed Emperor card asks, *How can I be less controlling?*

♦ EXTREMES ♦

The reversed card is the energy of the upright card taken too far. **EXAMPLE:** The Ace of Swords is about focus and clarity. The reversed Ace of Swords is about being overly focused in one direction and ignoring other possibilities.

JOURNALING IDEAS

The journal pages are designed with a dot grid so you can draw, sketch, or write. There are no rules for using this journal in your tarot practice! But if you'd like a little guidance, here are some ideas.

♦ PROMPTS ♦

Pull one card each day. Use the card as your prompt or intention for the day. Reflect on its meaning and write about it (see the Reference Pages, a glossary of each card and its meanings).

♦ QUESTIONS ♦

Ask your deck a specific question about what's going on in your life. The journal also includes a few lists of themed questions about relationships, creativity and work, clarity, and decision making. Pull a single card for each question and follow up with more cards if clarification or detail is needed. Use this journal to record your questions and answers.

♦ SPREADS ♦

A spread tells a more detailed story using tarot; it acts as an outline and the cards fill in the details. Each position within a spread defines that card's relationship to the other cards, and to the bigger picture. Choose a spread from page 96, 128, or 16 or create your own. Use this journal to record the story told by your chosen spread.

REFERENCE PAGES

The set of keywords and descriptions on the following pages is based on the Rider-Waite-Smith tradition, but most decks will correspond with these meanings to some degree.

If you'd like to come up with your own interpretations, or if you are using an oracle deck that has its own distinct vocabulary and structure, use some of the blank pages in this journal to record your observations for each card. Defining card meanings in your own way will personalize your tarot experience and add depth to your readings.

♦ SUITS, NUMBERS & COURT CARDS ♦

Once you know what each suit, number, and court position signifies, you can read almost any deck intuitively. This method works for playing cards as well as tarot.

ACE
A SEED · A BEGINNING

2
DUALITY · DIALOGUE
CHOICE

3
CREATION · FAMILY
GROUP DYNAMICS

4
STABILITY · STRUCTURE
FOUNDATION

5
CHANGE · IMBALANCE

6
COOPERATION · COMMUNITY
COMMUNICATION

7
POSSIBILITY · DISCOVERY
SPIRITUALITY

8
CYCLES · PATTERNS
REPETITION

9
IDEALISM · EXPECTATION

10
RESOLUTION · COMPLETION

COURT CARDS can refer to character traits, people who have these traits, or energetic influences.

Court cards are not indicators of gender; anyone can take on or be represented by the attributes of Pages, Knights, Queens, and Kings. The court cards are placed here in ascending playing card order, but you can decide your own hierarchy (if any). Modern decks often assign different roles to the court cards altogether.

PAGES are associated with inexperience; they are the students or apprentices of the deck.

KNIGHTS are fighters and agents of change; they represent action and forward motion.

QUEENS are open-minded and intuitive leaders or mentors.

KINGS are rule-based and methodical leaders or mentors.

WANDS	COINS	CUPS	SWORDS
PLAYING CARD SUIT CLUBS	**PLAYING CARD SUIT** DIAMONDS	**PLAYING CARD SUIT** HEARTS	**PLAYING CARD SUIT** SPADES
ELEMENT FIRE	**ELEMENT** EARTH	**ELEMENT** WATER	**ELEMENT** AIR
THEME PASSION & CREATIVITY	**THEME** THE PHYSICAL WORLD	**THEME** EMOTION & INTUITION	**THEME** REASON & INTELLECT
COGNITIVE FUNCTION INTUITION	**COGNITIVE FUNCTION** SENSATION	**COGNITIVE FUNCTION** FEELING	**COGNITIVE FUNCTION** THINKING

THE MAJOR ARCANA

THE FOOL

FREEDOM · FEARLESSNESS · INNOCENCE

Tarot is sometimes referred to as "the fool's journey." The cards in a tarot deck depict every aspect of human experience and development, and the Fool encounters the symbols on each card throughout their journey. They meet life's ups and downs with a sense of openness, possibility, and the freedom to make mistakes. The Fool is about potential; anything can happen.

Many tarot decks depict the Fool as a newborn. Children have a fearlessness and curiosity that adults often lose touch with as they get older. They make surprising connections and question rules that adults take for granted. The Fool is associated with play and childlike enthusiasm. Sometimes we figure out a much better way to do something when we don't know the "right" way to do it.

- How can I be more playful and less fearful?
- How can I trust my instincts?
- What journey is about to begin? How can I meet it with an open mind?

THE MAGICIAN

SKILL • TRANSFORMATION • POWER

The Magician represents a transformation that is within our control. In a reading, we can reflect on the importance of intention; sometimes the biggest transformational challenge is figuring out what we want. Once that is known, we may find that we have the will and the necessary tools to make it happen. Many Magician cards illustrate this concept with all four suits of tarot placed on a table. The suits are representations of the four alchemical elements: earth, fire, air, water.

The Magician has a deep sense of purpose and is determined to create lasting, significant change. He does this by channeling both internal and external energy. The Magician acts as a conduit between the spiritual and material worlds and embodies the Hermetic concept "as above, so below."

- What transformation is within my control?
- What tools are at my disposal?
- How can I act as a conduit for change?

THE HIGH PRIESTESS

INTUITIVE KNOWLEDGE • TRUTH
MEDIATION OF OPPOSITES

The earliest known tarot deck refers to the High Priestess as the Papess, or female pope. It is said that the card was inspired by a legend from the Middle Ages of a woman who became pope by disguising herself as a man. This is what the High Priestess card is about on a deep level: serving some higher cause by trusting our own truth.

The High Priestess is often connected to the Moon and its phases, which represent mystery and intuition. Another common image is of the High Priestess as a central figure positioned between two columns, light and dark. She holds a scroll, representing knowledge, and appears as a door between light and shadow.

- How can I mediate light and shadow?
- What is my deepest intuition telling me?

THE EMPRESS

FERTILITY • RESPONSIBILITY TO NATURE ABUNDANCE

The Empress is tarot's mother archetype. The Empress is a nurturer and embodies the metaphorical concepts of pregnancy and birth. This card is about taking responsibility for our world and environment and responding to our caring and protective nature.

How do we create and nurture something new? How do we bring the seed of an idea to fruition? When we pull the Empress card, we should use our emotions and instinct as a guide. We should follow our heart first and foremost.

- What am I nurturing or caring for?
- What is coming to fruition?

THE EMPEROR

WISDOM • EXPERIENCE • CONTROL

In The Pictorial Key to the Tarot, *A. E. Waite describes the Emperor as "embodied will." When the Emperor appears in a reading, we may need to take charge and exert influence over a situation. The ram is a traditional symbol of authority and willpower and often appears in illustrations of the Emperor.*

The Emperor is tarot's father archetype. This card can represent a fair and trustworthy leader but can also indicate the misuse or overuse of power.

- ♦ What is my relationship to authority?
- ♦ How do I exert influence?
- ♦ Where do I need more order or structure? Where do I need less?

THE HIEROPHANT

TRADITION • ETHICS • SPIRITUAL AUTHORITY

The word hierophant comes from ancient Greek and refers to a spiritual leader who has direct access to the mysteries of the afterlife. The hierophant is an intermediary between humanity and higher knowledge. In early tarot decks, this card was called the Pope. The Hierophant is about hierarchy, tradition, and institutions. When this card comes up in a reading, we could consider our place within these frameworks. How do we choose who to listen to and who to learn from?

Traditions are passed on for good reason; often, the most commonly traveled paths are the best ones. However, we can still follow tradition without being led blindly by it, adapting customs to fit our needs.

- ♦ How can I benefit from having or being a mentor?
- ♦ Who do I lead and who do I follow?
- ♦ Which traditions have real meaning and which ones do I follow out of habit or obligation?

THE LOVERS

LOVE · BEAUTY · UNION

The Lovers card signifies meaningful, consequential relationships—equal partnerships that make us feel strong and balanced. Although this card is typically associated with romantic relationships, the Lovers can refer to any kind of healthy relationship; friendships, work relationships, family, or creative collaborators, just to name a few. There is a feeling of wholeness and harmony here, open communication and a shared vision create a sense of "being in this together."

- Are my relationships guided by shared visions? What are these common themes?
- What qualities are important in a partnership?

THE CHARIOT

MOMENTUM • TRIUMPH • BREAKTHROUGH

The Chariot card is about action and pursuit. It often depicts a figure harnessing the power of two beings, one dark and one light. Sometimes they are horses. Sometimes they are sphinxes, lions, or swans. But they always represent two opposing forces being steered in the same direction. The Chariot represents a victory that is achieved by harnessing and directing opposing instincts or desires.

- What different directions am I being pulled in? How can I steer more confidently?
- What victory am I driving toward? What propels me forward?

STRENGTH

OVERCOMING DESIRE · BUILDING TRUST · COURAGE

In the earliest known tarot decks, Strength is illustrated by the myth of Heracles killing the Nemean lion, but the courage represented in modern decks has less to do with outward displays of force. Courage is the result of a subtle inner balance, a healthy attitude toward fear and a confidence that comes from self-knowledge. The Strength card has come to represent inner strength; encompassing the qualities of faith, loyalty, and patience.

The lion commonly illustrated in modern tarot decks represents passion and wildness. A tamed lion indicates overcoming a controlling instinct, harnessing it in purposeful way.

- What instincts do I want to control? What fears must be overcome?
- How can I learn to trust myself fully? How can I earn trust from others?

THE HERMIT

RETREAT • INTROSPECTION • SELF-CARE

The Hermit asks us to examine the role of solitude and self-discipline in our lives. There is value in observing thoughts and feelings away from outside influences and in learning to enjoy our own company. The Hermit is often depicted as a figure carrying a lamp—representing knowledge—through the darkness. This card can be about loneliness, isolation, and retreat, but it can also represent freedom and independence.

- How can I become a better observer of my own thoughts and feelings?
- What are the positive and negative aspects of being alone? How can I benefit from solitary reflection?

THE WHEEL OF FORTUNE

CHANGE • PLANS SET IN MOTION • KARMA

The Wheel of Fortune is about forward motion. This could mean putting a plan into action or, on a larger philosophical level, this card may remind us that all situations in life are fleeting. The Wheel of Fortune is a reminder that change is the only constant. Life is full of ups and downs; sometimes we're at the top of the wheel and sometimes we're getting crushed by it. This image is a cautionary tale about pride with a karmic aspect: "What goes around comes around."

- Where am I on the wheel at this moment? In what ways is this position temporary?
- What plans or ideas can I set in motion?

JUSTICE

REASON • FAIRNESS • LAW

The Justice card is about truth and objectivity. This card usually depicts scales, alluding to ethics, impartiality, and systems of law and order. It asks us to take a balanced, realistic, and honest view of events. Justice reminds us to distinguish between feeling and thought, between intuition and evidence, and to pause and find balance before we make a decision.

- ♦ What decision must be made?
- ♦ What deserves a fair and honest assessment?

THE HANGED MAN

PEACE • SELF-DISCIPLINE
FREEDOM FROM DISTRACTION

One way to interpret the Hanged Man is to think about the benefits of meditation: peace of mind, connection to the universe and humanity. Meditation pulls us out of our entrenched mindset and helps us transcend it. We might come back to our everyday concerns with a new perspective once we've had a chance to step away.

A word that often comes up for the Hanged Man is "crossroads." If we are trying to make a decision, this card could be asking us to have patience and faith that a solution will present itself. The Hanged Man represents a liminal state and an opportunity to pause and look inward.

- Where do I find stillness?
- What crossroads have been reached?

DEATH

CYCLES • DESTRUCTION • RENEWAL

Though it seems ominous on the surface, the Death card is about change and renewal. In contrast to the Magician, which illustrates change that is within our control, Death represents naturally occurring change that we either embrace or learn to accept.

Thinking about death as transformation can open a pathway toward acceptance. In literal and metaphorical terms, decay is necessary to fertilize new growth.

- What phases or cycles are ending? What new growth is possible?
- What changes are taking place?
- What feelings about change must be acknowledged or expressed?

TEMPERANCE

BALANCE • MODERATION • PATIENCE

To temper one thing with another is to create balance. In doing so, we neutralize any negatives that come from leaning too heavily toward one extreme. It can be difficult to take the middle path. Life is full of nuance and gray areas; very few things are black and white. When Temperance appears in a reading, think about what feels like "too much" and look for opposing actions that create balance. Consider what it would mean to hold two opposing things at the same time.

- What are the benefits of taking the center path or neutral position?
- What feels balanced?
- Where is temperance needed?

THE DEVIL

TEMPTATION · ATTACHMENT · CONTROL

The Devil traditionally signifies materialism and attachment. In Buddhist, Hindu, and other Eastern philosophies, attachment is considered the source of all suffering. When we fixate on something we desire, we allow it to take control. This card could signify a need to be in control, or a feeling of being controlled—by another person, habit, situation, commitment. When perspective is limited, we may feel trapped.

The Devil can signify desires overpowering judgment and self-defeating patterns of behavior. This card is often associated with addiction or other forms of unhealthy dependence.

- What habits are no longer working for me?
- What do I feel a need to control? What is controlling me?

THE TOWER

REVELATION • DISASTER • A SHIFT IN PERSPECTIVE

The Tower represents a moment of realization that changes everything. Imagine building a tower on a shaky, uneven foundation. This image evokes a sense of impending doom, perhaps related to a goal we've been working toward, a relationship we've developed, or a project we have nearly completed. It can feel terrible to start over, but sometimes it is the only way to move forward.

The Tower does not represent a complete loss, however. The experience of starting over can help to rebuild in a more honest and informed way. The Tower illustrates the necessity of seeing through our own delusions. We may confront a problem on our own or be forced to do so by circumstance.

- What truths must be acknowledged?
- What tensions must be confronted?

THE STAR

FAITH • HOPE • HEALING

The Star is about possibility and trusting the universe. This card is about finding a purpose; about having faith that you are doing the right thing, at the right time. It brings to mind the phrase "wishing on a star." Sometimes a wish can point us in the right direction because it gives us a goal to aim toward.

In the sequence of the Fool's journey, the Star comes after the Tower; it represents the moment after the dust clears and our position becomes clear. To find a "north star" is to discover a sense of direction. The Star is a guiding light, a comfort, and a relief.

- What is my "north star" at this moment?
- What am I wishing for?

THE MOON

SUBTLETY • MYSTERY • INSTINCT

The Moon is tied to emotions, dreams, the subconscious, and the imagination. Since the moon does not radiate its own light as the sun and stars do, its natural state is darkness. Lunar phases, as we see them, are dependent on reflected light from the sun. The Moon exists in a state of darkness, shadow, and ambiguity and at the same time, it silently controls the tides on earth. This card is a reminder to fully experience our feelings and to seek emotional truth. Don't just rely on clearly defined answers. The Moon asks us to look beyond our immediate perception and search for deeper meaning.

- ♦ What are my instincts telling me?
- ♦ What feelings or dreams need analysis?
- ♦ What am I unsure about? How can I accept ambiguity?

THE SUN

HEALING · CLARITY · NEW LIFE

The Sun card is about "shedding light" and seeking truth. While the Moon represents the unconscious, the Sun represents consciousness. It is warm, radiant, and uncomplicated; nothing is hidden.

Apollo, the Greek sun god, is also the god of truth, healing, and medicine—which makes sense, as the sun is the source of all life on earth. When the Sun appears in a reading, we can consider what elements are essential in order for new growth to take place.

- What brings clarity?
- What is essential?

JUDGMENT

RECKONING • AWAKENING • AN ANNOUNCEMENT

As the second to last card in the Major Arcana, Judgment signals a time for making assessments, acknowledging truth, and taking responsibility. The openness and wholeness of the last Major Arcana card, the World, is the result of truthful analysis and decision making. Judgment is a reminder that real change is possible only after we have taken an honest look at the present and the past.

This card often has religious overtones and represents the idea of "judgment day," when souls are sorted into heaven or hell. This card represents an announcement at the start of a new day.

- Where in my life can I take responsibility?
- How can I forgive or ask forgiveness?

THE WORLD

WHOLENESS • PEACE • OPEN-MINDEDNESS

In her book Seventy-Eight Degrees of Wisdom, *Rachel Pollack refers to the World as "the unconscious known consciously." This card represents the freedom to live honestly, with a solid understanding of our place in the world. When our inner and outer selves are aligned, we feel at home anywhere. We are grounded in reality but able to access what is beyond our immediate perception.*

This final card in the Major Arcana also signifies a beginning. The World represents a new perspective on reality that is informed by the lived experience of the cards preceding it.

- What brings me peace?
- What makes me feel at home in the world?
- How can I be more open-minded?

THE MINOR ARCANA

ACE OF WANDS

CONFIDENCE, CONVICTION, EMPOWERMENT

In tarot, aces represent beginnings; wands symbolize passion and creativity. The Ace of Wands combines single-pointed clarity with fire and intensity. Take initiative and wield your strength and passion purposefully.

- What passion motivates me?
- What are my strongest convictions?

TWO OF WANDS

CREATIVE PARTNERSHIP, A WELCOME CHALLENGE, DECISIONS

Like two sticks rubbed together to start a campfire or the intensity between individual people, groups, or ideas, this card represents powerful forces that fuel one another, for better or for worse. Consider the process of getting to know someone through agreements and disagreements. This card could also represent the process of figuring out what works for a particular creative project or weighing options based on some internal conflict.

- What challenges are welcome?
- What internal or external debates are taking place?

THREE OF WANDS

EFFORTS REWARDED, SUCCESS IN BUSINESS, PROGRESS

Passion is needed at the earliest stages of starting something new, whether it's a creative endeavor, a business project, or a relationship. Put in the effort and you will find a specific kind of success that comes from planning and strategy. Once the basic groundwork is completed, a new project or experience is free to take on a life of its own.

- How do I build a foundation for myself? How can I grow beyond it?
- In this moment, what planning and/or strategy is necessary?

FOUR OF WANDS

SOLID FOUNDATIONS, STABILITY, CELEBRATION

This is your reminder to be flexible and rooted, like the upright, sturdy branches often depicted on this card. The 4 of Wands is at once a call for ritual and celebration and a reminder of the importance of stability. Often illustrated with a wedding, this card represents a union that contributes to the greater good. The foundations we create for ourselves can extend to our community as well.

- What bonds form my foundation? How do I extend that foundation beyond myself?
- How can I celebrate those who provide support?

5

FIVE OF WANDS

PLAY, COMPETITION MINOR CONFLICT

Change or imbalance may contribute to a creative struggle. There may be an intensity to this challenge, but the tone is light and unserious. Conflict and competition may provide the training needed to move forward.

- What is my relationship to competition?
- How can I learn from play and grow from conflict?

6

SIX OF WANDS

VICTORY, SUCCESS ANTICIPATION

The classic interpretation of this card is victory, but there is also a subtle, somber note to the Rider-Waite-Smith 6 of Wands card, which depicts a thoughtful figure on a horse. The rider is either heading to or returning from battle. The joyfulness of victory exists alongside the heaviness of "getting back in the saddle." A victory may bring celebration but may also increase expectations from others.

- What victory can be celebrated?
- What changes can success bring?

7

SEVEN OF WANDS

VIGILANCE, A STRUGGLE TO STAY AHEAD

When presented with a challenge in which you have the upper hand, remain active, aware, and persistent. This challenge may be internal, creative, or spiritual. Closely examine what you have to gain or lose. Having a full awareness of the situation may naturally increase vigilance or cause you to question the meaning of your struggle.

- What requires persistence?
- Am I experiencing a stalemate? What would help put an end to it?

8

EIGHT OF WANDS

REPETITION, SWIFT MOVEMENT TO CREATE STABILITY, INTENTIONALITY

Harness your energy and focus on the moment when you know exactly what needs to be done. Take action in the most expedient way possible. The 8 of Wands illustration by Pamela Colman Smith depicts eight wands flying through the air like arrows heading toward a target. Archers may appear to hit the target effortlessly, but their confidence is the result of sustained effort and practice.

- What expertise have I gained through practice? How can I apply it?
- What goal is motivating me?

9

NINE OF WANDS

ANTICIPATION
PREPARATION, DEFENSE

The 9 of Wands is about persistence and resilience, especially when your strength has been tested and you are close to the finish line. As a result of past struggles, you may have developed a realistic awareness of the challenges ahead. Awareness may sometimes lead to an overabundance of caution. When your guard is up, you anticipate having to defend yourself. The key is to be prepared without becoming defensive.

- What am I anticipating?
- How can I be prepared, rather than defensive?

10

TEN OF WANDS

A RESPONSIBILITY
BURDEN, HARD WORK

You may have accumulated more responsibility than you can handle. Perhaps a creative project has gone beyond its original scope or a relationship has become more emotionally demanding than expected. Are you working too hard or taking on too much? Are you moving at an unsustainable pace? Determine what is essential to avoid burnout. Set boundaries, ask for help, and assess the emotional cost before over committing.

- Am I taking on too much?
- What is essential, and what can I leave behind?
- Should I ask for help? How can I ease the burden of others?

PAGE OF WANDS

CURIOUS, ENTHUSIASTIC INNOVATIVE

Having more enthusiasm than experience can be a great asset; innovation often happens when we want to do something but don't have the right tools. The dark side of this is overconfidence, arrogance, and pushing forward without the necessary knowledge. Mediate these coexisting aspects by making an honest assessment of what you don't know and asking for help.

- What am I most enthusiastic about at this moment?
- How can uncertainty be an asset? When should I ask for guidance?

KNIGHT OF WANDS

DETERMINED, TENACIOUS CHARISMATIC

Knights are fighters and agents of change. Personified by fire and charisma, the Knight of Wands is someone who pushes forward no matter the cost—one who is impulsive, and at times explosive or unreasonable.

- How do I fight for what I'm passionate about?
- What requires tenacity?

QUEEN OF WANDS

WARM, CONFIDENT, STRONG

With the fiery optimism of the Sun and the inner fortitude of Strength, the Queen of Wands is a magnetic, self-assured person who knows when to show restraint and when to be vulnerable. Project confidence and connect deeply with others while maintaining your unique perspective.

- What helps me project warmth and confidence?
- How can I motivate others?
- How can I lead creatively?

KING OF WANDS

IDEALISTIC, BOLD, TRANSFORMATIVE

The King of Wands has a bold vision and can transform something from one state into another, as fire does. The King of Wands is a person with the power and vision to shape their surroundings, like a teacher or a healer.

- How can I be an agent of tranformation?
- How can I shape the world around me?

ACE OF CUPS

EMOTIONAL, SPIRITUAL, OR CREATIVE FLOW

A state of flow is overwhelming, but in the most positive sense. Think about the times that you've been lost in a creative project, times when work doesn't feel like work, or when love or spirituality offers an overall sense of well-being. These feelings often come about at the start of something new; nurture them.

- What feels natural and easy?
- What helps me experience a state of flow?

TWO OF CUPS

EQUAL PARTNERSHIP, RECIPROCITY, CONNECTION

A relationship or partnership that is based on mutual respect allows for the equal flow of emotion in all directions. This relationship may not be romantic—it could refer to a particularly balanced friendship or business partnership. This union of two forces who put in equal effort is a collaboration that works well.

- What constitutes an equal partnership?
- How can I can add balance to my relationships?

THREE OF CUPS

CELEBRATION, COMMUNITY, CREATIVITY

Whether your family is biological or chosen, here is an outpouring of emotion shared with your loved ones. A party is the simplest way to read this card, but on a deeper level it is about friendship, platonic love, and shared experience. Celebrate victories and accomplishments with the people closest to you. Reconnect with those you care about.

- What victories deserve recognition and celebration?
- What loved ones should I reconnect with?

FOUR OF CUPS

HESITATION, FEAR OF REPEATING PAST MISTAKES, REEVALUATION

It is easy to fall into a sense of apathy or complacency when movement and flow have stabilized. Or perhaps a perception of the present is colored by past failures. The danger of this card is when we become so focused on past disappointments that we are unable to see potential in front of us.

- What mistakes or disappointments are holding me back?
- How do I remain open to new opportunities?

5

FIVE OF CUPS

LOSS, LETTING GO, ACCEPTANCE

Grieving, loss, or emotional struggle can be internal or external. When things are not going as planned, step back and assess your approach. At the same time, it is important to acknowledge that meaningful change and growth often come from disappointment.

- How can I accept a loss?
- How can I make the best of a difficult situation?

6

SIX OF CUPS

NOSTALGIA, LONGING, INNOCENCE

When we idealize the past, truth is often obscured by our limited memory. You may remember people or events in stark black and white—as either all good or all bad. The 6 of Cups is about nostalgia and revisiting your childhood innocence, as well as the idea of passing something on to the next generation.

- What brings feelings of nostalgia?
- What memories can I pass on?

7

SEVEN OF CUPS

SECRETS, IMAGINATION, NEW FEELINGS

There are positive and negative aspects of fantasy. When something is new and unknown, the sense of possibility inflates. This card is also a reflection on the nuanced differences between imagination and delusion.

- What feels new and exciting?
- What is unknown?

8

EIGHT OF CUPS

DISSATISFACTION, UNCERTAINTY, DOUBT

Are you searching for something beyond what you've already attained? The Rider-Waite-Smith 8 of Cups card uses the moon eclipsing the sun as a metaphor to suggest that rationality is being eclipsed by instinct. We may not know what we're looking for, but we know it's there.

- What is creating dissatisfaction?
- What am I looking for?

9

NINE OF CUPS

SELFISHNESS, EXCESS, SATISFACTION

Receive too much of what you want and it may be a good time to share wealth, responsibility, or feelings to avoid becoming overwhelmed. Selfishness and excess can be negative qualities, but a degree of selfishness is sometimes necessary. Excess can be seen as abundance, but even success can be too much to manage alone.

- What do I have too much of? What can I share?
- Is selfishness harmful or necessary?

10

TEN OF CUPS

CONTENTMENT, AFFIRMATION, HARMONY

The pursuit of "happily ever after" provides a sense of happiness, contentment, and warmth. This card is often illustrated with a rainbow—a reminder that all life situations are fleeting. Appreciate the good times while they last.

- What makes me feel complete? What feels resolved?
- What can I appreciate in the present moment?

PAGE OF CUPS

IMAGINATIVE, INTUITIVE, TEMPERAMENTAL

The Page of Cups is learning to understand your own emotions. This person is a dreamer; someone who easily gets lost in their own imagination. Find a way to take on these qualities or look to someone who has them for inspiration.

- How can I learn to trust my own feelings?
- What are my instincts telling me?

KNIGHT OF CUPS

CHARMING, SEDUCTIVE, DRAMATIC

The Knight of Cups is an agent of change and a fighter—a person who creates drama. In other words, this person uses emotion to persuade people or influence events.

- How do I use emotion to influence or persuade?
- Who am I charmed by, or drawn to?

QUEEN OF CUPS

NURTURING, EMPATHETIC, ARTISTIC

The Rider-Waite-Smith Queen of Cups sits on the land, but her feet are in the ocean. She connects to her feelings but stays grounded. This approach informs her artistic process and makes her a kind and empathetic leader.

- How can I be an empathetic leader?
- How can I be both resolute and receptive?

KING OF CUPS

SENSITIVE, INVENTIVE, RESOURCEFUL

The King of Cups is a keen observer of the world around him. He is an artistically or scientifically inclined person who is able to channel feelings into innovative solutions.

- How does my sensitivity help me professionally or artistically?
- How can I channel my emotions productively?

ACE OF SWORDS

FOCUS, CLARITY, NEW IDEAS

The Ace of Swords encourages bold choices. The sword, upright in absolute truth, cuts through all that is unnecessary to find what is essential. The danger here is when we become overly fixated on reason, ignoring feelings and intuition. Life is full of gray areas, but sometimes we need to define things in absolutes to avoid indecisiveness.

- What gives me clarity? What helps me focus?
- What bold decision must be made?

TWO OF SWORDS

EQUILIBRIUM, MUTUAL RESPECT, INDECISION

A balance of intellect between equals either leads to mutual loyalty and respect or creates an impasse. This card could indicate a weighing of two choices and is sometimes illustrated with a blindfolded person balancing two swords. What information are you unable to see? A decision may become easier once you factor in intuition, instead of relying on reason alone.

- What intellectual dialogue is taking place?
- What choices am I weighing?

THREE OF SWORDS

SORROW, HEARTBREAK, INTROSPECTION

Look at your family or other group dynamics with an intellectual distance. Traditionally illustrated with three swords through a heart, this card encourages us to accept our pain. Feeling and acknowledging sorrow is an essential part of moving beyond it.

- How can reason and intellect help with emotional difficulties?
- What sorrow must be felt and acknowledged?

FOUR OF SWORDS

REST, RECUPERATION, SOLITUDE

Rest and stillness offer time to gather strength. Perhaps an intellectual regrouping is in order. Perhaps there is a great loss to mourn. Give yourself time to gather and restructure your thoughts to form a new foundation and outlook.

- Are rest and recuperation needed now?
- What am I gathering strength for?

5

FIVE of SWORDS

DISAPPOINTMENT, DEFEAT, A DIFFICULT OPPONENT

Winning or losing does not always look the way we expect it to. An intellectual challenge may be a chance for disappointment, but it may also yield an unexpected outcome or an opportunity to grow. The difficult opponent we face may be something within.

- ♦ What potential disappointments am I facing? How can I reframe my expectations?
- ♦ What am I struggling with? How can I adjust my strategy?

6

SIX of SWORDS

LEAVING WORRIES BEHIND, TRANSITION, RITE OF PASSAGE

Rational decision making may move you toward a place of easier communication or a greater feeling of belonging and safety. Reflect on a chosen passage from one place to another and seek out a welcoming community.

- ♦ What am I looking forward to? What am I moving toward?
- ♦ What should I keep and what should I leave behind?

SEVEN OF SWORDS

INNOVATION, WIT, DUPLICITY

Make connections between disparate things to solve problems in unusual ways. Think outside the box. The shadow side of this card, however, reveals duplicity, sneakiness, or victory by underhanded means.

- What requires an innovative solution?
- How do I resist duplicity or betrayal (in myself or from others)?

EIGHT OF SWORDS

RUMINATION, STAGNATION, IMPRISONMENT

What fears hold you back? The 8 of Swords may indicate repetitive or unproductive thought patterns. Until you observe your situation with clarity and without fear, you may believe you are helpless.

- What am I dwelling on?
- What thoughts, fears, or choices are holding me back?

9

NINE OF SWORDS

RUMINATIONS, NIGHTMARES, A STRUGGLE TO MAKE SENSE OF EVENTS

When expectations and intellect collide, you may realize your ideal outcome is unlikely. Something feels uncomfortable, but you may not yet know what it is. Situations feel extreme in these moments of helplessness, but once you are fully awake, the anxiety dissipates.

- What worries me? How can I put my concerns into perspective?
- How can I reassess my expectations?

10

TEN OF SWORDS

SURRENDER, RELEASE, AWAKENING

An intellectual confrontation. An acceptance of truth. In the Rider-Waite-Smith deck, Pamela Colman Smith illustrates a face-down figure impaled by ten swords with a sunrise in the distance. The figure has nothing left to do but accept their fate, but a new day beckons. The 10 of Swords represents an awakening, earned by experiencing each of the challenges before it.

- What surrender is necessary? What awakening is on the other side of it?
- What do I need to accept?

PAGE OF SWORDS

CAREFUL, OBSERVANT, VIGILANT

The Page of Swords hesitates to take action because of their inexperience. Instead of meeting opposition head-on, they seek out different perspectives and observe from a distance. This card can signal either a need for caution or an overabundance of it.

- What new information am I waiting for?
- Is caution helping or holding me back?

KNIGHT OF SWORDS

INQUISITIVE, CRITICAL, ANALYTICAL

An aggressive seeker of knowledge, the Knight of Swords can easily cut through all that is unnecessary to get to the heart of the matter.

- What requires investigation or analysis?
- How can I cut through what is unnecessary?

QUEEN OF SWORDS

PRINCIPLED, STRATEGIC, AMBITIOUS

The Queen of Swords is a strategic leader with a sense of purpose, someone determined to live by their principles. Like religious and mythological figures who acknowledge the dark realities of the world, these leaders are courageous, and live by their own truth. Here is someone who is straightforward, loyal, and brave.

- What are my strongest convictions?
- What are my ambitions? How can I assess them strategically?

KING OF SWORDS

AUTHORITATIVE, IMPARTIAL, PRECISE

The King of Swords signifies an emotionally detached leader who upholds laws and traditions. Emotional distance and objectivity makes for a tough but fair decision-maker. The King of Swords values precision and respects hierarchy.

- How can I be a fair and objective leader?
- How much should I follow or enforce existing rules and hierarchies?

ACE OF COINS

ESTABLISHMENT OF ROOTS, CULTIVATION, OPPORTUNITY

A seed in its humblest form will take on whatever form its environment allows. A traditional reading of this card may indicate financial opportunity, but this card is about establishing roots. On an elemental level, it is crucial to cultivate your environment to make it more conducive to growth.

- What ecosystem am I a part of? How do I contribute to it?
- What roots am I putting down?
- How can I make my environment more conducive to growth?

TWO OF COINS

JUGGLING MULTITASKING, INTERDEPENDENCE

Juggle multiple things at once and a dialogue between them opens up. This is often illustrated with the two coins inside of a figure 8 or an ouroboros, indicating a duality that is ongoing and ever present. Two things are kept in motion by their interdependence.

- What ongoing duality is present? How are its components interdependent?
- What am I juggling?

THREE OF COINS

CRAFTSMANSHIP, SUCCESSFUL COLLABORATION, ADMIRATION

Some goals really can't be accomplished alone. Remember to ask for help and to appreciate the unique skills and abilities of the people around you. Pamela Colman Smith illustrates this card with an artist, an architect, and a religious leader admiring a stained-glass church window, collaborative work that serves a greater purpose.

- What do I have to contribute?
- When should I ask for help?
- What work feels most meaningful?

FOUR OF COINS

SECURITY, FRUGALITY, PREOCCUPATION WITH MATERIAL POSSESSIONS

Hold on tight to what you have—but not too tight. Sometimes it is necessary to protect your assets. Boundaries are essential, but it is important to not close off entirely or to refuse help to someone who needs it. When we lock others out, we may be locking ourselves in as well.

- Where should I draw a boundary?
- When can I let my guard down?
- How can I protect what I have?
- How can I let others in?

5

FIVE of COINS

HUMILITY, NEED, SURVIVAL

One manifestation of physical or material instability is a need for more than we have. Accepting help and paying dues can both be humbling experiences.

- What help or assistance is needed?
- What dues must be paid?

6

SIX of COINS

CHARITY, HARMONY, COOPERATION

Share resources with friends and neighbors and make sure everyone has what they need. What do you contribute to the greater good of the community when you bring something to the communal table?

- How am I dependent on my friends and community? How do they depend on me?
- What is the value of shared experience?

7

SEVEN OF COINS

PATIENCE, TRUST, PROGRESS

The 7 of Coins is the waiting period after a seed has been planted, when growth is just beginning. Your efforts will be rewarded through care and patience. Here is a reminder to assess your progress and trust the process.

- What progress is being made?
- What requires patience?

8

EIGHT OF COINS

COMFORT, HARD WORK, PERSISTENCE

It takes discipline to practice, learn, and master a new skill. When you are fully absorbed in work, your attention is focused on the process rather than the end result. You may be creating something meaningful, or the act of work itself may take on spiritual significance.

- What work can I get lost in? What labor is meaningful?
- What do I want to learn?
- What skills or traditions can I pass on?

NINE OF COINS

SELF-SUFFICIENCY, SECURITY, ACCOMPLISHMENT

Appreciate your achievements. Trust yourself without a need for outside opinions. Enjoy a sense of peace, knowing that what you have is enough. In contrast to the 10 of Coins, this is a solitary contentment.

- What security can I create for myself?
- What can I accomplish on my own?

10

TEN OF COINS

SECURITY OVER RISK, ENJOYMENT OF WEALTH

With harmonious relationships and stability comes a feeling that everything has fallen into place. Wealth abounds and not just material wealth but family, friendships, and community support. Another aspect of this card is intergenerational harmony; the sharing of knowledge and experiences with those who are older or younger than we are. Continuity of experience creates a stable community.

- What constitutes health? What do I need to feel content?
- How can I connect meaningfully with older and younger generations?

PAGE OF COINS

DILIGENT, FASCINATED, SCHOLARLY

The Page of Coins is an apprentice who is learning by working diligently at their craft. As students of science and reality, they are learning to appreciate the world as it is.

- What fascinates me? What do I want to learn?
- How can I observe and accept things as they are?

KNIGHT OF COINS

PRACTICAL, EXPEDIENT, ECONOMICAL

The Knight of Coins pushes for the most efficient course of action and has no patience for frivolity or excess. They are trustworthy and purposeful with money, resources, and time.

- What is the most practical course of action?
- How am I too efficient?
- How can I allow space for experimentation or outside influence?

QUEEN OF COINS

RECEPTIVE, NURTURING, INVENTIVE

The Queen of Coins is firmly rooted in reality. They feel at home anywhere, making those around them feel comfortable. This card illustrates self-awareness as well as ingenuity, the ability to work with the materials at hand. The Queen of Coins is a scientist, a nurturer, and an explorer.

- How can I work with the materials that are available to me?
- How can I increase my self-awareness?

KING OF COINS

DISCIPLINED, GENEROUS, CONTENT

The King of Coins has earned a sense of security through hard work and realizes the true value of their wealth. Instead of being constrained by it, the King of Coins shares wealth with others and contributes to the greater good. The King of Coins is grounded in reality but finds peace in their connection to something greater than themselves: humanity, spirituality, nature, community.

- How can I shift my perspective to see the bigger picture?
- How can I help others and contribute to the greater good?

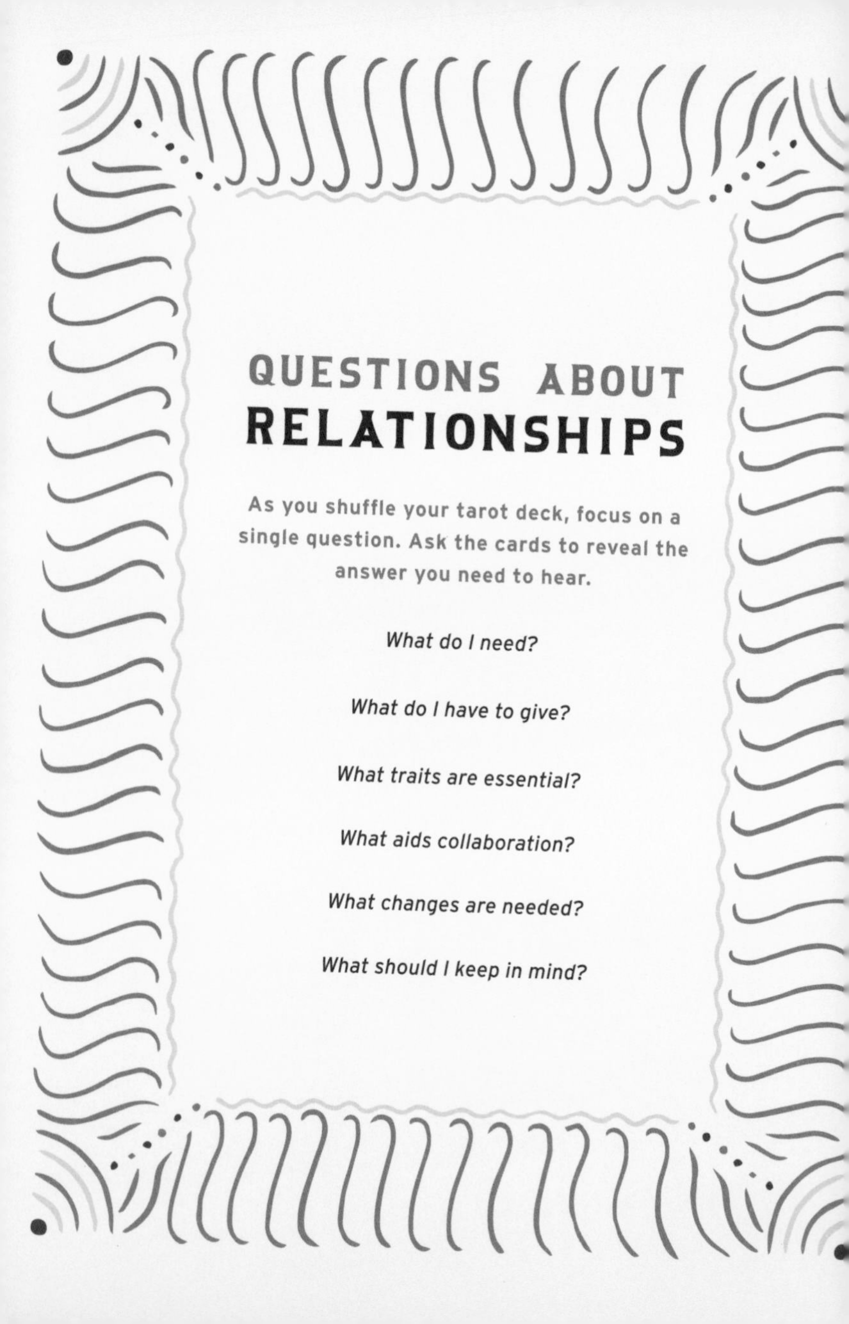

QUESTIONS ABOUT RELATIONSHIPS

As you shuffle your tarot deck, focus on a single question. Ask the cards to reveal the answer you need to hear.

What do I need?

What do I have to give?

What traits are essential?

What aids collaboration?

What changes are needed?

What should I keep in mind?

SPREADS

Here are a few simple spreads for daily journaling.

♦ SPREAD FOR TODAY ♦

Choose three cards to represent your day. Place them in a row to represent, from left to right: *Morning, Afternoon, Evening*.

♦ BRIDGE ♦

Select four cards. Place the first three in a row, and the fourth card horizontally across the center card. The first three represent (from left to right): *Challenge, Obstacle, Outcome*. The fourth horizontal card represents a *Lesson*.

♦ PYRAMID ♦

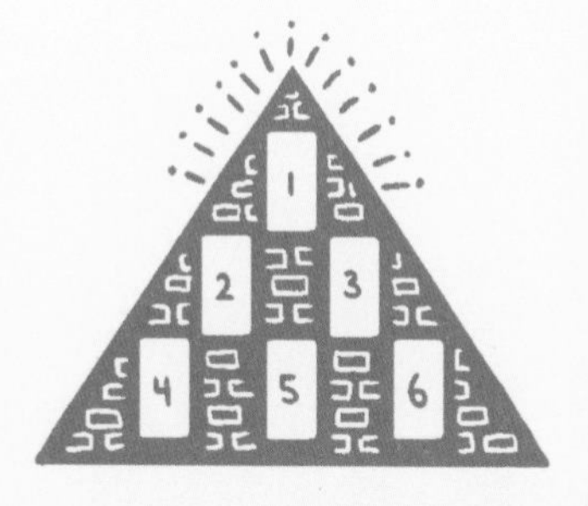

Place one card down to represent a *Goal*. Place two cards below it to represent the Inner Resources you have that will help you reach it. Place three cards below that to represent *Outer Resources*—in other words, the support you seek or receive from external sources (family, friends, environment, community, and the like).

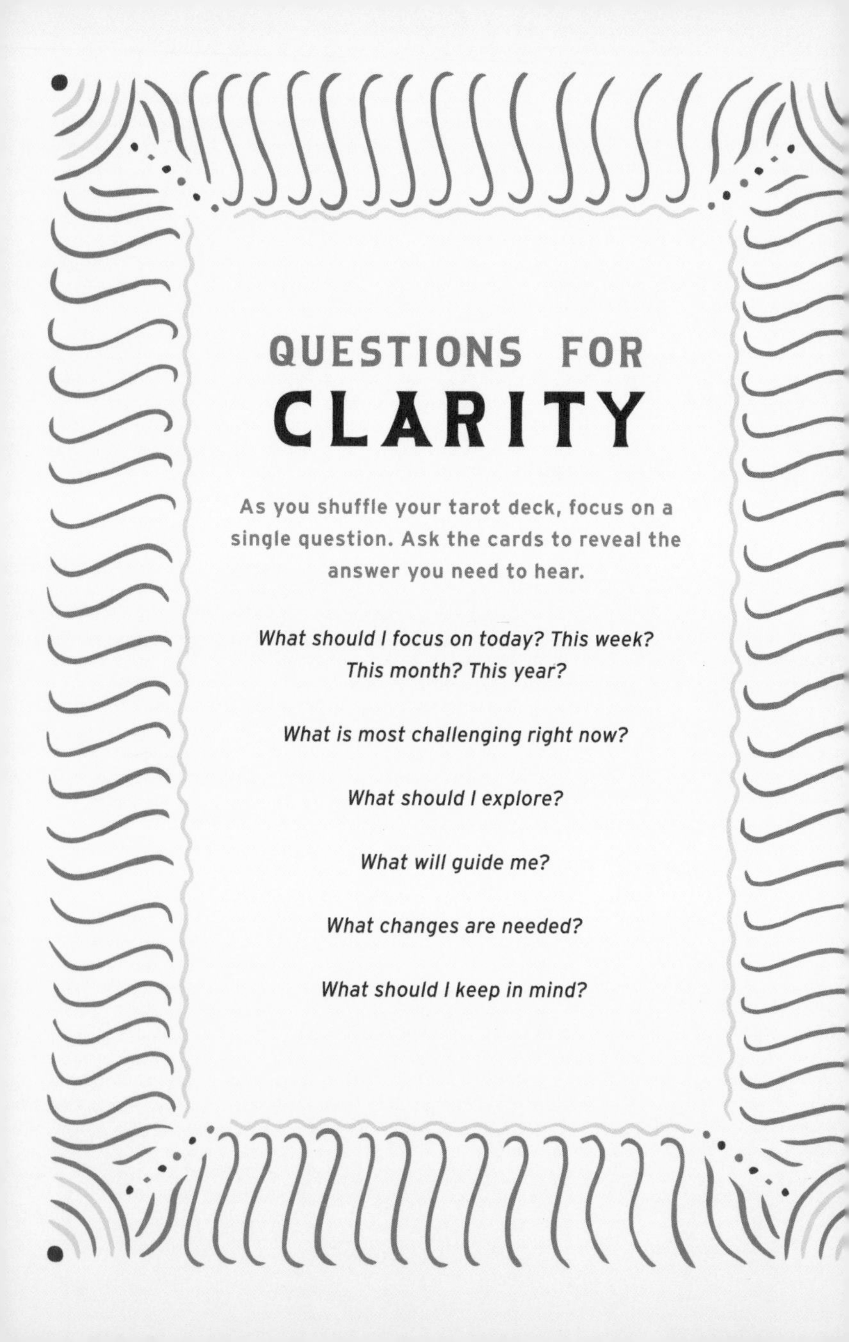

QUESTIONS FOR CLARITY

As you shuffle your tarot deck, focus on a single question. Ask the cards to reveal the answer you need to hear.

What should I focus on today? This week? This month? This year?

What is most challenging right now?

What should I explore?

What will guide me?

What changes are needed?

What should I keep in mind?

SPREADS

Here are a few simple spreads for daily journaling.

♦ REFLECTION ♦

Select two cards and place them vertically, one on top of the other. The top card represents our *Outer Landscape* (what the world sees) and the bottom card represents our *Inner Landscape* (subconscious feelings).

♦ SHADOW ♦

Select two sets of three cards and place them in two horizontal rows. The first column represents The Past (top card) and The Past: Shadow (bottom card). The second column represents The Present (top) and The Present: Shadow (bottom). The third column represents The Future (top) and The Future: Shadow (bottom).

♦ THIRD EYE ♦

Select two cards and place them next to each other. These are *The Left Eye* and *The Right Eye* (two cards that, together, represent a single point of view). Select a third card and place it horizontally and centered above the two *Eye* cards. This card is *The Third Eye* (insight).

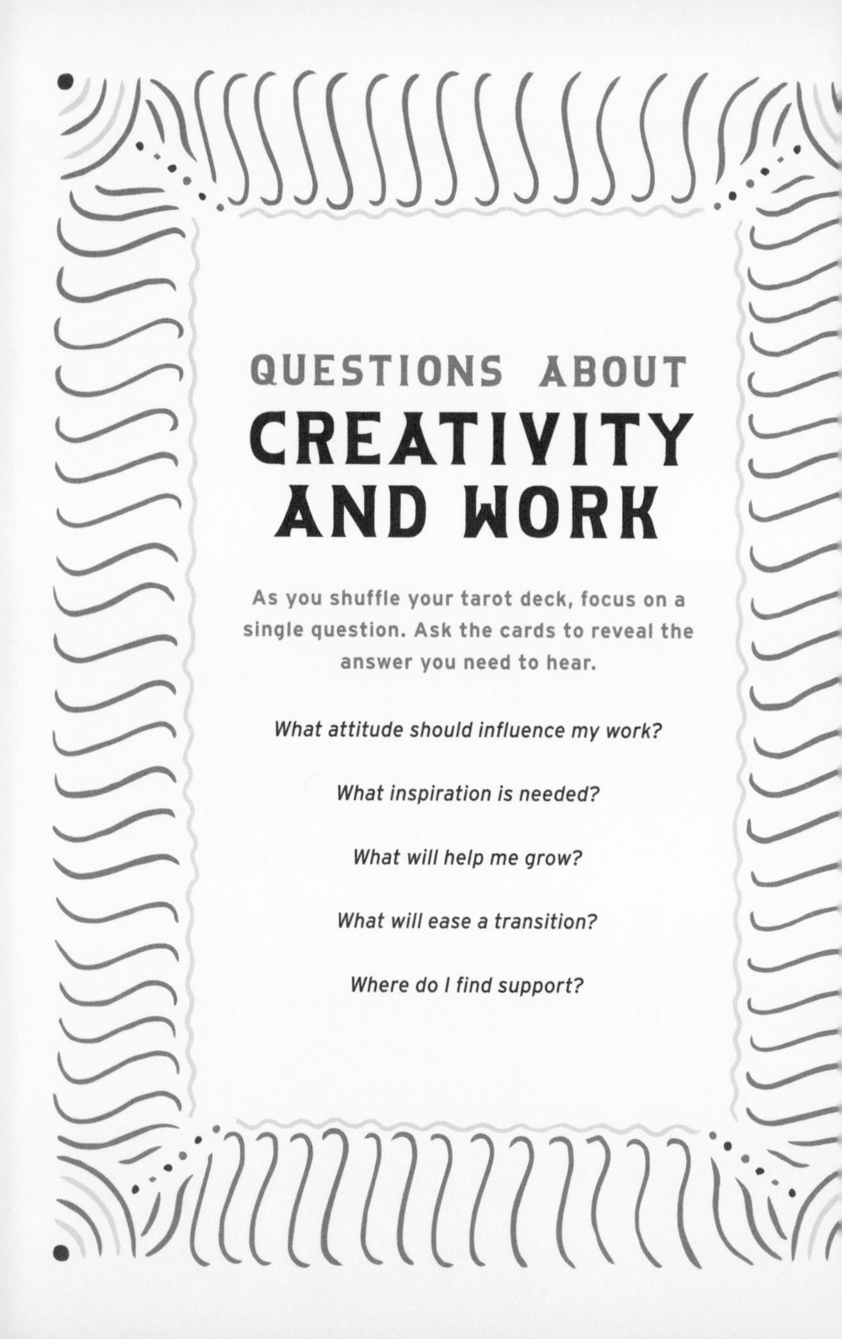

QUESTIONS ABOUT CREATIVITY AND WORK

As you shuffle your tarot deck, focus on a single question. Ask the cards to reveal the answer you need to hear.

What attitude should influence my work?

What inspiration is needed?

What will help me grow?

What will ease a transition?

Where do I find support?

SPREADS

Here are a few simple spreads for daily journaling.

♦ TOWER ♦

Select five cards and lay them out vertically, one on top of the other. The bottom card is Card 1, representing the *Subconscious/Feelings*; Card 2 represents *Foundation/Support*; Card 3, *Consciousness/Thoughts*; Card 4, *Outlook*; and Card 5, *Reach*.

♦ RELATIONSHIP SPREAD ♦

Select as many cards as there are people in the relationship. I'm using the term *relationship* as broadly as possible because this spread works not only for a love relationship but also for families, coworkers, friends—anyone. Assign each card to a *Person* as they are turned over. Then choose a final card to represent the *Relationship* as a whole.

♦ CREATE YOUR OWN ♦

In her book *Tarot for Your Self*, author Mary K. Greer suggests creating your own tarot spreads based on a specific question you'd like to answer. Since a tarot spread works like an outline, one way to do this is to break down a big question into components and then assign a card (or a set number of cards) to each component.

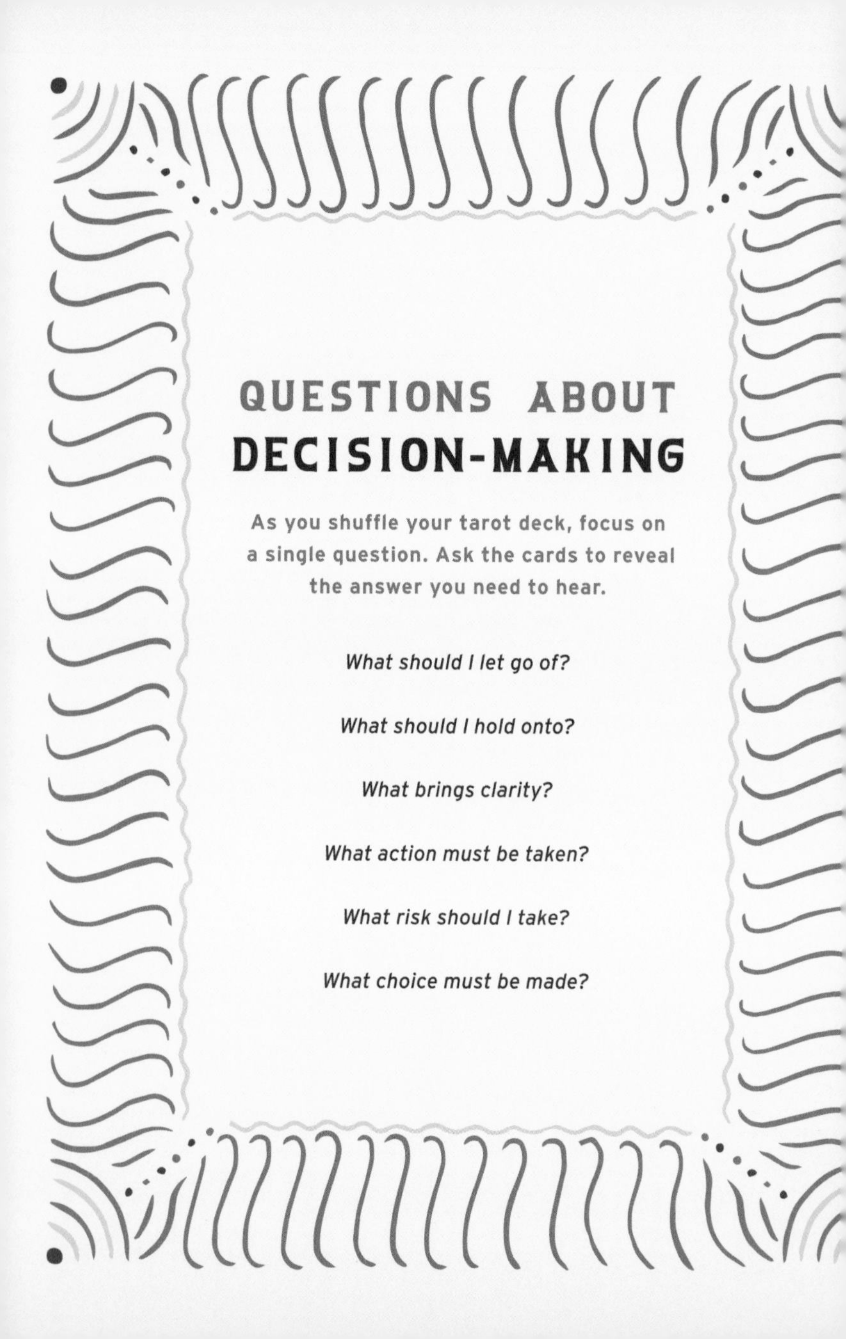

QUESTIONS ABOUT DECISION-MAKING

As you shuffle your tarot deck, focus on a single question. Ask the cards to reveal the answer you need to hear.

What should I let go of?

What should I hold onto?

What brings clarity?

What action must be taken?

What risk should I take?

What choice must be made?

SUGGESTED READING

The following books were my most trusted and relied-upon resources in learning about tarot and creating this journal. If you are looking to further expand your tarot knowledge, I highly recommend checking these out.

Holistic Tarot: An Integrative Approach to Using Tarot for Personal Growth BY BENEBELL WEN (2015)

Queering the Tarot BY CASSANDRA SNOW (2019)

Seventy-Eight Degrees of Wisdom: A Book of Tarot BY RACHEL POLLACK (1986)

Tarot and Psychology: Spectrums of Possibility BY ARTHUR ROSENGARTEN, PHD (2000)

Tarot for Your Self: A Workbook for Personal Transformation BY MARY K. GREER (2002)

Published in the United States by Clarkson Potter/
Publishers, an imprint of Random House,
a division of Penguin Random House LLC, New York.

CLARKSONPOTTER.COM

CLARKSON POTTER is a trademark and POTTER
with colophon is a registered trademark
of Penguin Random House LLC.

ISBN 978-0-593-13984-4

Printed in China

Illustrations by Caitlin Keegan
Design by Lise Sukhu

3 5 7 9 10 8 6 4 2

First Edition

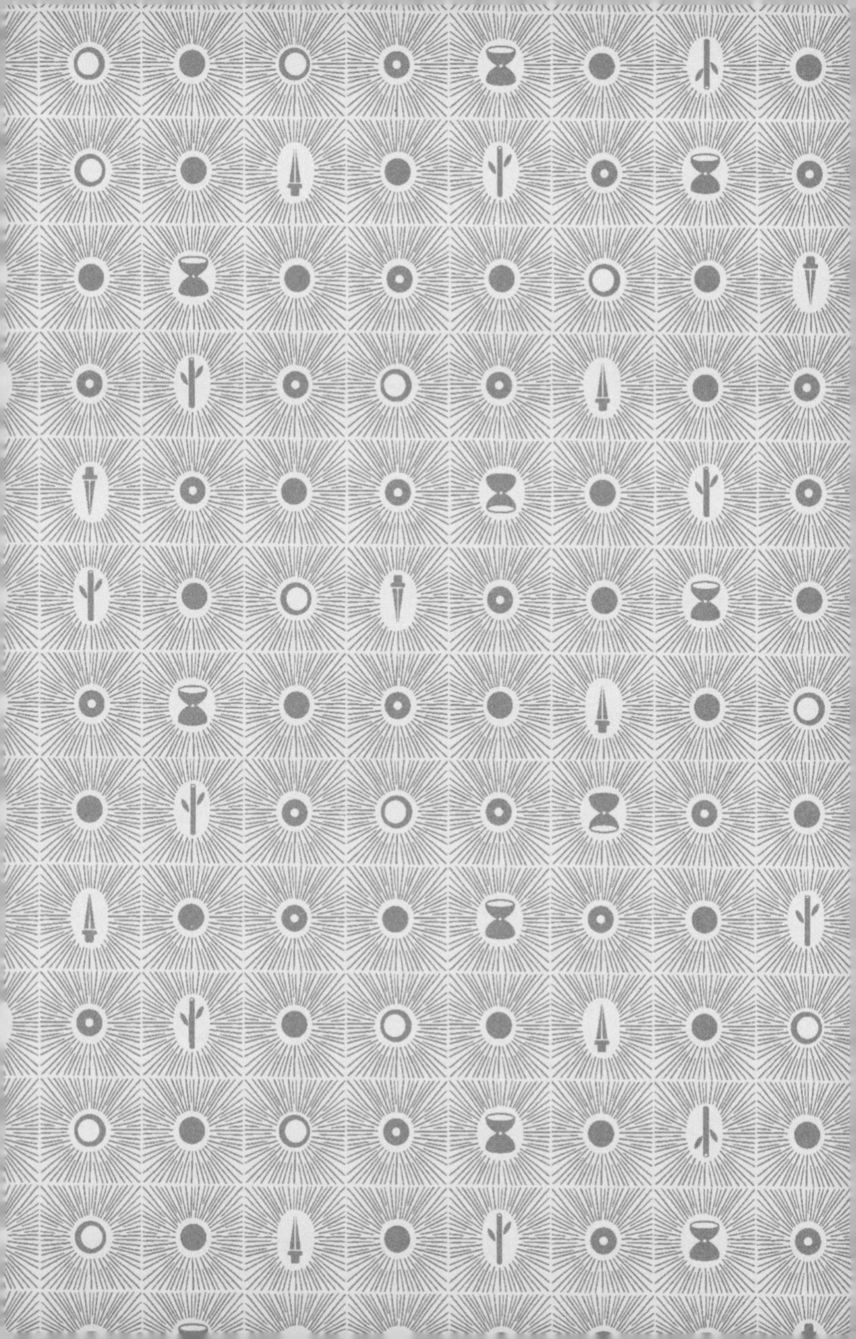

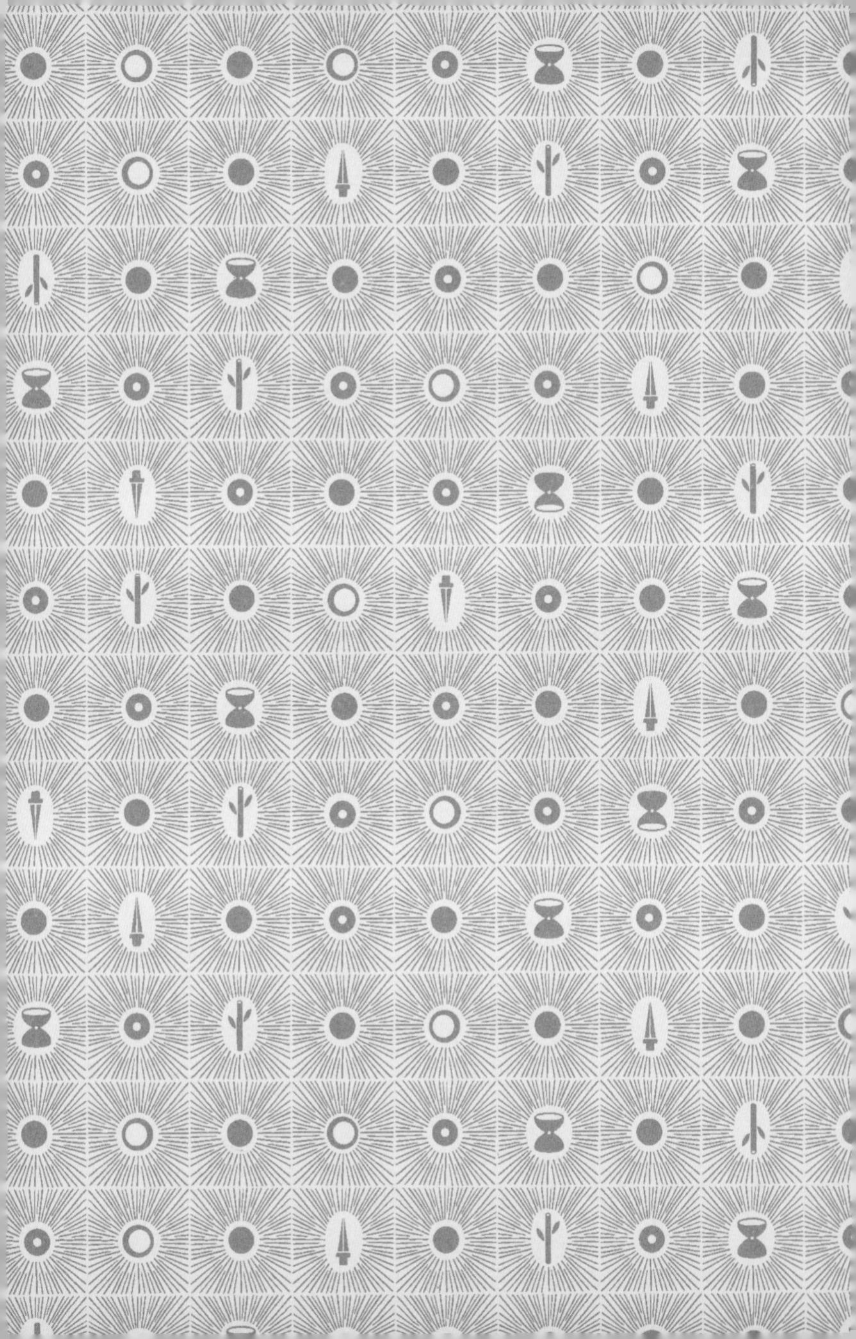